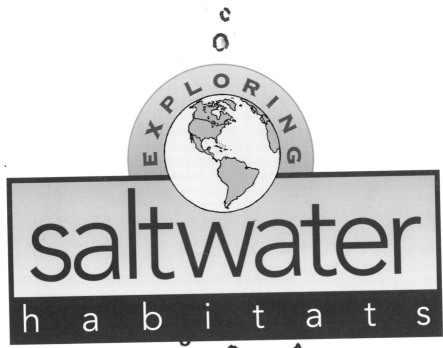

EXPLORING

saltwater

h a b i t a t s

SMILE

Written by Sue Smith

Wildlife illustrations by Cynthia A. Belcher

Cartoon illustrations by Miriam Katin

MONDO

Emperor penguins page 20

Sea otter and kelpfish page 7

Giant tube worms and octopus page 11

Sheepshead fish page 9

Contents

Velvet crab page 16

Green sea turtle page 4

Coral reefs

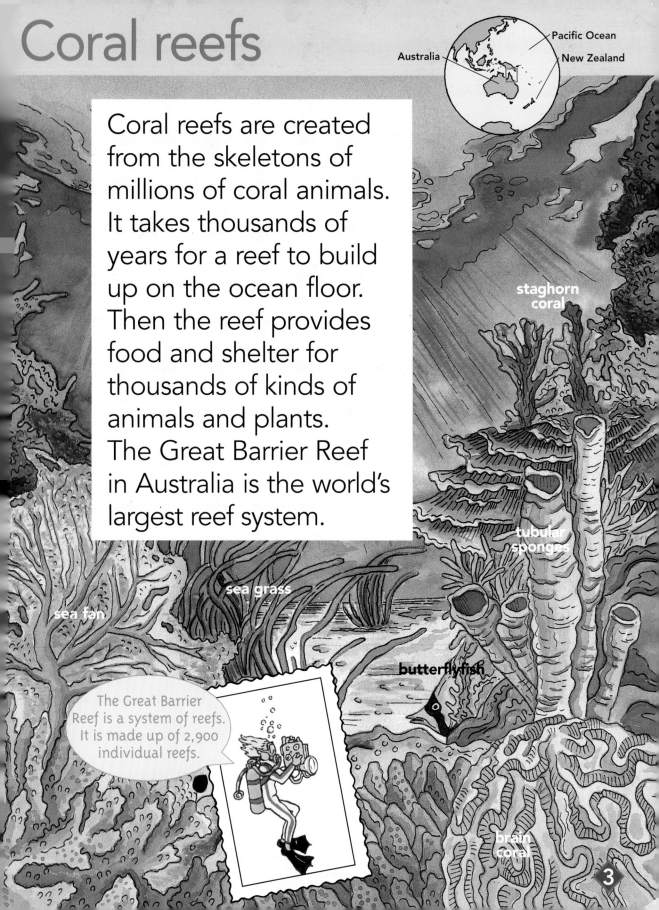

Australia — Pacific Ocean — New Zealand

Coral reefs are created from the skeletons of millions of coral animals. It takes thousands of years for a reef to build up on the ocean floor. Then the reef provides food and shelter for thousands of kinds of animals and plants. The Great Barrier Reef in Australia is the world's largest reef system.

staghorn coral

tubular sponges

sea grass

sea fan

butterflyfish

The Great Barrier Reef is a system of reefs. It is made up of 2,900 individual reefs.

brain coral

Tubular sponges filter tiny bits of food from the water they pump through themselves.

green sea turtle

humpback whale and calf

A black-backed butterflyfish uses its pointed snout to pick among coral, looking for food.

The candy sea cucumber ejects sticky threads to distract and annoy its enemies.

blue sea star

biscuit sea star

4

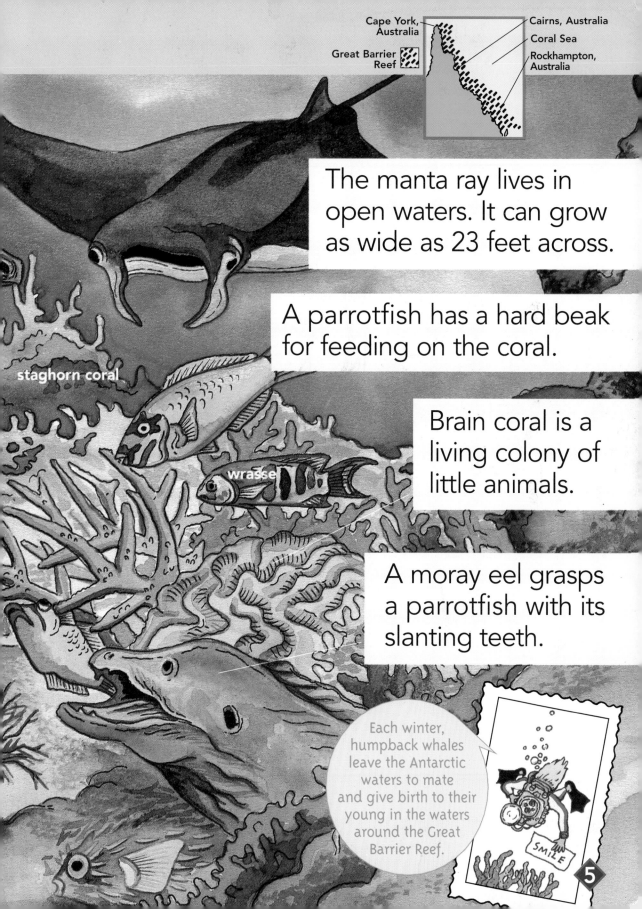

The manta ray lives in open waters. It can grow as wide as 23 feet across.

A parrotfish has a hard beak for feeding on the coral.

staghorn coral

Brain coral is a living colony of little animals.

wrasse

A moray eel grasps a parrotfish with its slanting teeth.

Each winter, humpback whales leave the Antarctic waters to mate and give birth to their young in the waters around the Great Barrier Reef.

SMILE

Life cycles

The life cycles of some reef animals take place entirely in the sea. The life cycles of others occur both on land and in the sea.

Green Sea Turtles

1. After mating: On a moonlit night, a female turtle digs a nest in the sand and lays 50 to 150 soft-shelled eggs.

2. Later that night: She throws sand over the nest to hide the eggs, returns to sea, and mates again.

3. For the next 42 days: Babies grow with their soft-shelled bodies folded in half.

 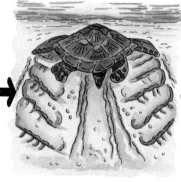 

  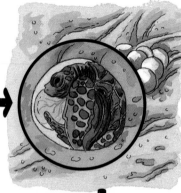

6. 20 to 40 years of age: The turtle grows slowly to adulthood but can weigh as much as 400 pounds.

5. The first night after hatching: They burrow out of the nest and scramble to sea.

4. On day 43: They hatch, weighing 1 ounce each.

In the past, female green turtles have laid more than 1 million eggs at one beach on one night. But because people eat turtle eggs and adult turtle meat, green turtles are endangered now.

6

CAN YOU FIND IT?

Turn back the page and find the porcupinefish.

Kelp forests

Kelp is a kind of seaweed that grows up from the rocky bottom of the ocean and spreads across the water's surface. Giant kelp forests grow in the Pacific Ocean, off the western coast of North America. Kelp forests are major habitats for smaller plants and hundreds of animals.

sea otter

kelpfish

Garibaldi

Giant kelp has been known to grow as tall as 130 feet, nearly as tall as the Statue of Liberty in New York. The statue is 151 feet and 1 inch high.

canopy

Sea otters live near the water's surface, but they swim to the ocean bottom for food.

seal

mid-water

Spanish shaw

sea lion

This kelpfish lives down deeper. Its brownish-purple coloring camouflages it against the darker fronds.

floor area

swell shark

A wolf eel catches a crab with its powerful jaws and eats it, shell and all.

swell shark egg case

Pacific Ocean

San Francisco, California, U.S.A.

kelp forests

Anchorage, Alaska, U.S.A.

Vancouver, Canada

Mexicali, Mexico

The kelpfish that lives in the canopy is golden brown and blends with the surface kelp.

rockfish

male

juvenile

female

Sheepshead fish change colors and gender as they grow.

holdfast

The sea otter wraps itself up in kelp and sleeps floating on its back in the kelp. The kelp keeps it from washing away with the waves.

A giant sunflower star sits on top of its food when it feeds.

Life cycles

Animals like the swell shark use kelp in many ways during their life cycles. Kelp provides shelter, food, camouflage, and protection.

Swell Sharks

1. After mating: Adult female (1 to 4 feet long) lays two eggs, each wrapped in a leathery case.

2. For 240 days: Each young shark feeds on a yolk sac inside case.

3. Day 241: Young shark breaks open the case with two rows of big scales on its back.

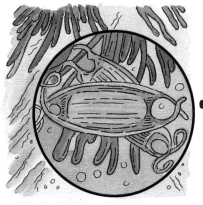
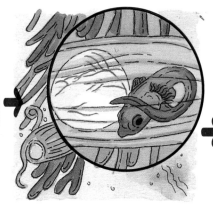

4. When the shark reaches 1 foot: It begins to lose those rows of big scales slowly as it grows to adulthood.

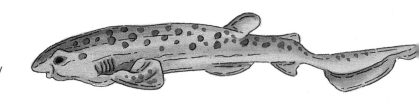

Although the leathery cases protect eggs before they hatch, about 65% of all eggs are still eaten by snails.

CAN YOU FIND IT?

Turn back the page and find the abalone.

Southeast Asia

Pacific Ocean

Australia

North America

Hawaii, U.S.A.

About three-fourths of our planet is covered with water, and most of that is dark, deep sea. The Pacific Ocean is one place where these deep waters can be found. Because they are so dark, many animals down there make a light of their own called bioluminescence.

giant tube worms

thermal vent

octopus

The deepest sea trenches in the world are the Marianas and Challenger deep trenches in the Pacific Ocean. They are each more than 35,000 feet deep, which is about 7 miles.

Lanternfish recognize other lanternfish by the light patterns on their bodies.

The swallower has an enormous mouth that can take in a whole fish and a stomach that can expand to hold it.

anglerfish

Some shrimp have lights on their heads to help them see their prey.

With special submersible vehicles, scientists can go far underwater to learn about animals living in the deep sea.

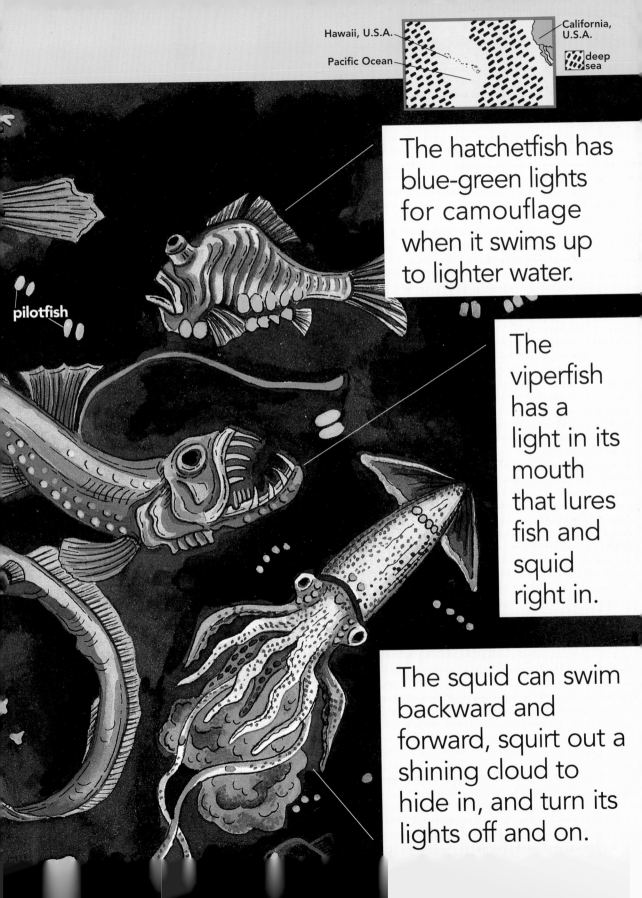

Hawaii, U.S.A.

Pacific Ocean

California, U.S.A.

deep sea

The hatchetfish has blue-green lights for camouflage when it swims up to lighter water.

pilotfish

The viperfish has a light in its mouth that lures fish and squid right in.

The squid can swim backward and forward, squirt out a shining cloud to hide in, and turn its lights off and on.

Life cycles

The stages of some deep-sea animals' life cycles occur at different depths of the sea.

Anglerfish

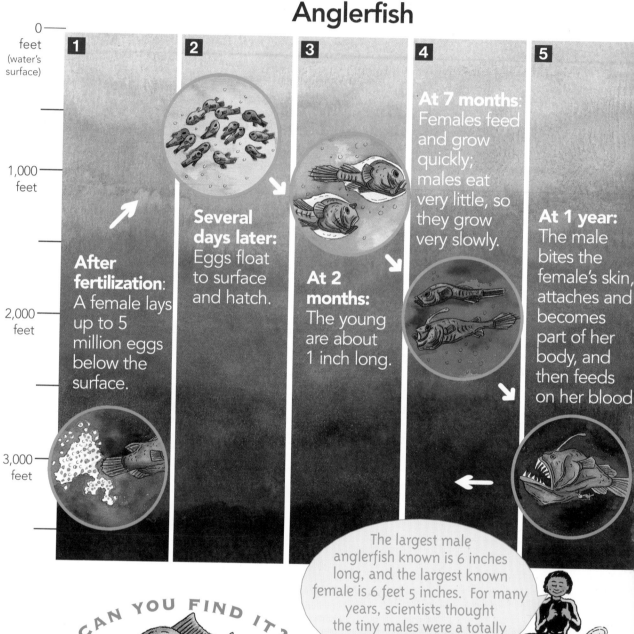

0 — feet (water's surface)

1,000 feet

2,000 feet

3,000 feet

1 **After fertilization:** A female lays up to 5 million eggs below the surface.

2 **Several days later:** Eggs float to surface and hatch.

3 **At 2 months:** The young are about 1 inch long.

4 **At 7 months:** Females feed and grow quickly; males eat very little, so they grow very slowly.

5 **At 1 year:** The male bites the female's skin, attaches and becomes part of her body, and then feeds on her blood

The largest male anglerfish known is 6 inches long, and the largest known female is 6 feet 5 inches. For many years, scientists thought the tiny males were a totally different kind of fish.

CAN YOU FIND IT?

14 Turn back the page and find the pilotfish.

Tide pools

Tide pools are holes surrounded by rocks and filled with water along the seashore. Waves wash over them two times a day. This changes the water temperature and brings fresh oxygen and food to the plants and animals that live in tide pools. They have adapted to these changes. Many tide pools dot the coast of Maine.

sea

arnacles

tide pool

seaweed

sea star

urchin

encrusting sponges

To eat a mussel, a sea star crawls over the mussel, and forces its stomach into the crack between the mussel's shells. It then eats the mussel inside.

rockweed

The sea anemone uses its stinging tentacles to push a small fish into its mouth. Then it holds onto the fish tightly with the suckerlike pad under its body.

These dog welk snails are eating barnacles. They can use their muscular feet to hold on or to move.

shanney

A velvet crab rears up on its back legs and holds out its sharp pincers to protect itself. It tucks itself under rocks to hide.

barnacles

rockweed

A cluster of mussels attaches itself firmly to rocks so that the waves do not wash it out of the pool.

A starfish holds fast with the suckers on its tube feet.

sea slugs

encrusting sponges

hermit crab

The velvet crab can grow a new leg if it breaks one. If it loses a claw protecting itself, it can grow a new claw, which may be even bigger than the one it lost.

A sea scorpion has a huge mouth that it can open wide to swallow smaller fish in one gulp.

Most animals that live in tide pools spend their whole live
there even though the tides wash in and out every da

Starfish

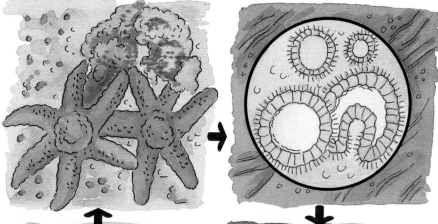

1. The first day: The adult female starfish sheds millions of eggs in a tide pool. The male starfish sheds sperm into the water.

2. End of first day: Eggs and sperm meet by chance and develop into larvae.

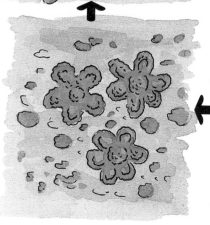

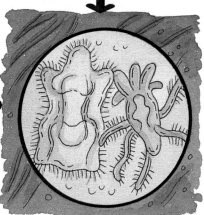

4. In about 2 months: The larvae settle to bottom of tide pool and attach to a rock or some other hard surface while growing into adults.

3. For 3 weeks: Larvae float in the sea as they feed and grow.

If a sea star loses all but one of its arms, it can regrow its missing arms gradually. Also, if a sea star is cut evenly in half, each half can regrow the missing half.

18

CAN YOU FIND IT?

Turn back the page and find the decorator crab.

Antarctica

South America
Africa
Antarctica
Australia

Antarctica is the vast area surrounding the South Pole. Glaciers, icebergs, sea ice, snow, and rocks are all part of this habitat. It is almost totally covered with ice in the winter. Yet a whole community of sea creatures inhabits this icy place and its waters.

glacier

iceberg

seals

There are NO polar bears and NO walruses in Antarctica. They live only in the Arctic.

krill

chin strap penguins

rocks

The humpback whale feeds on krill in the Antarctic summer.

Krill are a major food source for many Antarctic animals.

A male emperor penguin incubates an egg when winter approaches.

blue whale

gentoo penguin

Antarctic cod

squid

An Antarctic tern breeds in Antarctica and spends its entire life near the pack ice.

A leopard seal, usually alone, approaches two crabeater seals on the open ice.

crabeater seals

A Weddell seal breathes through a hole in the ice that it sawed with its teeth.

sand dollars

The blue whale is bigger than the largest dinosaur that ever lived. It can weigh 150 tons — as much as 88 cars. Its heart is the size of one small car.

sea stars

Life cycles

Although most Antarctic animals breed in summer, the emperor penguin breeds in winter.

Emperor Penguins

1. After mating: When female is 6 years old, she lays one fertilized egg on the ice. She does this every year from then on.

2. For 60 days: Egg is incubated on top of the male's feet, held in place beneath a flap of his feathered belly.

3. Day 61: Chick hatches.

6. At 4 years old: Penguin is a fully mature adult.

5. At 1 year old: Chick grows juvenile feathers and goes to open sea to feed.

4. For next 40 days: Fema keeps the chick warm and feeds it.

Hundreds of males incubating eggs form a huddle for protection from the cold. They pack together standing up, all facing the center and leaning inward. Each rests its beak on the shoulder of the bird in front of him.

CAN YOU FIND IT?

Turn back the page and find the sea cucumber.

Glossary

adapt - to change in order to survive a new or different environment.

bioluminescence - the light an animal makes.

breed - to produce young.

camouflaged - hidden because the animal's natural coloring blends into its surrounding environment.

canopy - the uppermost part of the water formed by kelp covering.

egg case - a flexible protective sack in which an egg develops.

fertilized egg - an egg that has combined with a sperm and can develop into an animal.

filter - to run water through in order to remove food or other particles.

frond - a large blade of seaweed that can make the plant's food.

glacier - a huge mass of ice that moves down a slope or across land very slowly.

habitat - the place where an animal or a plant lives.

holdfast - strands at the base of kelp that hold the plant securely to a surface.

iceberg - a large piece of ice that has separated from a glacier and floated out to sea.

incubate - to keep warm in order to hatch.

inhabit - to live in.

juvenile - young.

lure - something that is used to attract an animal.

mid-water - the level of water located between the ocean floor and surface level.

oxygen - a gas in both air and water that some living things need to live.

pack ice - layers of ice that begin at the surface and go down toward the bottom of the sea.

pincer - a part of the body used to grip or grasp.

prey - an animal that is killed by another animal for food.

scales - the flexible bony plates that cover the bodies of most fish.

seaweed - a water plant without stems, roots, or leaves. It is a kind of algae.

South Pole - the southernmost part of the Earth.

thermal vent - an opening in the deep ocean sea floor from which warm water spews into the cold waters.

Index